CRUISE CONTROL

DIET

Cookbook

Recipes to Help Automate Your Diet and Conquer Weight Loss Forever.

By

Laura Williams

ISBN-13: 978-1-950772-40-7
ISBN-10: 1-950772-40-3

Disclaimer:

The information provided in this book is designed to provide helpful information on the subjects discussed.

Table of Contents

INTRODUCTION:

The Cruise Control Diet

There are thousands of diet books on the market, and I think I must have read them all: low fat diets, low carbohydrate diets, low calorie diets, Paleo diets, keto diets. All of these diets work if you follow them carefully ... at least in the beginning. The pounds do not fly, but the balance is still moving in the right direction, just a little slower. Then more slowly. Then more slowly. But your happiness is short-lived. Because despite all your efforts, your weight starts to move upward. Slowly at the beginning. But with the increasing horror, you see that it is accelerating. In a year or two at the most, your weight has come back to all of these efforts to lose weight. You are crushed. You are devastated. You know that you have done your best, even if you face the silent accusations and the overwhelming condescension of your friends and family.

Again in the 1970s, before the epidemic of obesity. Look at an old picture of that time, maybe a street scene. What's amazing is how low obesity is. Take a look at some old high school yearbooks from the 1970s, there is virtually no obesity. Maybe a child in a hundred. The answer is: "They did not eat all the time". Large-scale surveys in 1977 showed that most Americans ate three times a day. Breakfast lunch and dinner. On the other hand, an average person eats at least six times a day for about fifteen hours. Think of it in concrete terms: this means that the average person has breakfast at 8:00. and do not stop eating until 10:45! The only time we do not eat is when we sleep. Grazing is good ... if you are a cow or want to look like one.

The physiology of weight gain is not that complicated. Your body really only exists in 2 states: the nourished state and the fasting state. When you eat (i.e. the fed state), insulin rises, which tells the body to store some of that incoming food energy as body fat. When you do not eat (fasting), insulin levels drop, which tells the body to use some of that stored food energy. We need it to feed our brain, our heart, our lungs, our kidneys, etc. Your body can store or burn fat, but not both at the same time.

In addition to all this, as this technique does not concern what you eat, it will work regardless of the style of diet you follow. From keto to vegan, you can use intermittent fasting to improve your body's ability to burn fat, lose weight and improve your health.

Furthermore, being careful when eating does not require any of us to restrict food groups, count points, track calories, or exercise for hours and hours. In other words, when you focus on the moment, you can automate your diet - you do not have to think about all these other criteria.

With healthy fats, you can still physically stay in a state of intermittent fasting that promotes weight loss, burning fat, but also energy and mood, without the slightest feeling of hunger and cravings that do hours of abstinence such a bitch (excuse my French). If you want to lose weight and improve your health as quickly and as little effort as possible, you will struggle to beat Cruise Control. My cruise control technique also works best because it increases the way proteins are processed in your body to help you build better muscles.

BURN ZONE BREAKFAST BEVERAGES

Ham Cheddar Chive Soufflé

NOTE: This makes a total of 5 servings.

Ingredients:

½ medium Onion (diced)

6 oz. Ham Steak (cooked and cubed)

6 large Eggs

1 cup of Cheddar Cheese (shredded)

2-3 tablespoons of Fresh Chives (chopped)

¼ teaspoon of Black Pepper

3 tablespoons of Olive Oil

1 ½ teaspoons of Garlic (minced)

1 tablespoon of Butter (to grease ramekins)

½ cup of Heavy Cream

½ teaspoon of Kosher Salt

Directions:

1. Meanwhile, you heat oven to 400F.
2. After which you heat olive oil in a pan and add onions.
3. Then, once soft, add garlic to brown.
4. Add all of the ingredients together in a bowl and mix well.
5. After that, you separate mixture into ramekins and bake for 20 minutes.
6. Finally, let cool slightly and serve.

Savory Sage and Cheddar Waffles

Ingredients:

3 teaspoons of baking powder

½ teaspoon of salt

2 cups of canned coconut milk

2 eggs

1 cup of shredded cheddar cheese

1 1/3 cup of coconut flour (sifted)

1 teaspoon of dried ground sage

¼ teaspoon of garlic powder

½ cup of water

3 Tablespoons of coconut oil (melted)

Directions:

1. First, you heat your waffle iron according to manufacturer's directions, at a moderate heat.
2. After which in a mixing bowl whisk together flour, baking powder, and seasonings.
3. After that, you add liquid ingredients, then stir until stiff batter forms.
4. Then you mix in the cheese.
5. At this point, you liberally grease top and bottom panels of the waffle iron, then place a 1/3-cup scoop of batter onto each iron section.
6. This is when you close the iron and cook until steam rises from the machine and the top panel opens freely without sticking to the waffle. (NOTE: proper cooking usually takes 2 cycles at moderate heat.)

White Pizza Frittata

Note: this makes a total of 8 servings of Keto White Pizza Frittata.

Ingredients:

9oz bag of Frozen Spinach

5 oz. of Mozzarella Cheese

½ cup of Fresh Ricotta Cheese

4 tablespoons of Olive Oil

Salt and Pepper (to Taste)

12 large Eggs

1 oz. of Pepperoni

1 teaspoon of Minced Garlic

½ cup of Parmesan Cheese

¼ teaspoon of Nutmeg

Directions:

1. First, you microwave frozen spinach for 3-4 minutes.
2. After which you squeeze the spinach with your hands and drain off as much water as you can; set aside.
3. Meanwhile, you heat oven to 375F.
4. After that, you mix together all of the eggs, olive oil, and spices.
5. Then add in the ricotta, parmesan, and spinach. (NOTE: when adding the spinach, break it apart into small pieces.)
6. At this point, you pour the mixture into a cast iron skillet, then sprinkle mozzarella cheese over the top.
7. This is when you add pepperoni on top of that.
8. Finally, you bake for 30 minutes. Remove from the oven, slice, and serve!

Low Carb Mock McGriddle Casserole

Note: this makes a total of 8 servings of Low Carb Mock Casserole.

Ingredients:

¼ cup of Flaxseed Meal

10 large Eggs

6 tablespoons of Walden Farms Maple Syrup

½ teaspoon of Onion Powder

Salt and Pepper (to Taste)

1 cup of Almond Flour

1 lb. Breakfast Sausage

4 oz. Cheese

4 tablespoons of Butter

½ teaspoon of Garlic Powder

¼ teaspoon of Sage

Directions:

1. Meanwhile, you heat oven to 350F.
2. After which you put a pan on the stove over medium heat, then add the breakfast sausage. **(NOTE:** break up while it's cooking.)
3. Then, in a separate bowl, measure out all dry ingredients (including cheese), then add the wet ingredients.
4. After that, you add 4 tablespoons of syrup and mix together well.
5. Furthermore, once the sausage is browned and somewhat crispy, add everything (including excess fat) into the mixture and mix again.
6. After which you line a 9x9 casserole dish with parchment paper and then pour the casserole mixture into the dish.
7. At this point, you use 2 tablespoons syrup drizzled over the top for extra maple flavour.
8. This is when you place in the oven and bake for 45-55 minutes.
9. Then, once done, remove from the oven and let cool.

10. Finally, you remove the casserole by holding on to the edges of the parchment paper and lifting out.

Breakfast Tacos

Ingredients:

6 large Eggs

3 strips of Bacon

Salt and Pepper (to Taste)

1 cup Mozzarella Cheese (shredded)

2 tablespoons of Butter

½ small Avocado

1 oz. Cheddar Cheese (shredded)

Directions:

1. First, you cook the bacon on a baking sheet with foil for about 15-20 minutes at 375F.
2. Then, while the bacon is cooking, heat 1/3 cup of mozzarella at a time on clean pan on medium heat for the shells.
3. After which you wait until the cheese is browned on the edges (about 2-3 minutes).
4. After that, you use a pair of tongs to lift the shell up and drape it over a wooden spoon resting on a pot. (NOTE: do the same with the rest of your cheese, working in batches of 1/3 cups.)
5. At this point, you cook your eggs in the butter, stirring occasionally until they're done.
6. This is when you season with salt and pepper.
7. Furthermore, you spoon a third of your scrambled eggs, avocado, and bacon into each hardened taco shell.
8. After which you sprinkle cheddar cheese over the tops of the breakfast tacos.
9. Finally, you add hot sauce and cilantro if you'd like!

Breakfast Pizza Waffles

Nutritional value:

Note: this makes a total of 2 Breakfast Pizza Waffles.

Each pizza waffle

Ingredients:

4 tablespoons of Parmesan Cheese

1 tablespoon of Psyllium Husk Powder

1 teaspoon of Baking Powder

Salt and Pepper (to Taste)

3 oz. of Cheddar Cheese

4 large Eggs

3 tablespoons of Almond Flour

1 tablespoon of Bacon Grease (or Butter)

1 teaspoon of Italian Seasoning (or spices of choice)

½ cup of Tomato Sauce (I prefer Rao's)

Pepperoni (it is optional)

Directions:

1. First, immersion blend all ingredients (except for tomato sauce and cheese) together until it thickens.
2. After which you heat your waffle iron and add half of the mixture.
3. After that, you cook until finished, then repeat.
4. Then you add tomato sauce (1/4 cup per waffle), and cheese (about1.5 oz. per waffle) on the top of each waffle.
5. Finally, you broil for 3-5 minutes in the oven. (NOTE: Optionally add pepperoni to the top of these.)

Bacon Cheddar Chive Omelets

Nutritional value:

NOTE: makes 1 serving of Bacon Cheddar Chive Omelets.

Ingredients:

1 teaspoon of Bacon Fat

1 oz. of Cheddar Cheese

Salt and Pepper (to Taste)

2 slices Bacon (already cooked)

2 large Eggs

2 stalks Chives

Directions:

1. First, you make sure all ingredients are prepped.
2. After which you heat a pan on medium-low with bacon fat in.
3. After that, you add the eggs, and season with chives, salt, and pepper.
4. Then, once the edges are starting to set, add your bacon to the center and let cook for about 20-30 seconds.
5. This is when you turn off the stove.
6. Finally, you add the cheese on top of the bacon and fold edges on top of the cheese like a burrito - holding the edges in place to use the cheese as a "glue".
7. Then you flip over and warm through on the other side.

Bacon Avocado Muffins

NOTE: this makes a total of 16 Avocado Bacon Muffins.

Ingredients:

5 Slices of Bacon

½ cup of Almond Flour

1 ½ tablespoons of Psyllium Husk Powder

4.5 oz. of Colby Jack Cheese

1 teaspoon of Minced Garlic

1 teaspoon of Dried Chives

Salt and Pepper (to Taste)

1 teaspoon of Baking Powder

5 large Eggs

2 tablespoons of Butter

¼ cup of Flaxseed Meal

2 medium Avocados

3 medium Spring Onions

1 teaspoon of Dried Cilantro

¼ teaspoon of Red Chili Flakes

1 ½ cup of coconut Milk (from the carton)

1 ½ tablespoons of Lemon Juice

Directions:

1. First, in a bowl, mix together eggs, almond flour, spices, flax, psyllium, coconut milk and lemon juice.
2. After which you leave to sit while you cook the bacon.
3. Then in a pan over medium-low heat, cook the bacon until crisp.
4. After that, you add the butter to the pan when it's almost done the cooking.

5. You chop the spring onions and grate the cheese.
6. At this point, you add the spring onions, cheese, and baking powder; crumble the bacon.
7. This is when you add the crumbled bacon and melted butter to the batter.
8. Furthermore, slice an avocado in half, remove the pit, and then cube the avocado while it's in the shell. (NOTE: Be careful of the sharp knife as you do this.)
9. After that, you scoop out the avocado and fold into the mixture gently.
10. Meanwhile, you heat oven to 350F, measure out batter into a cupcake tray that's been sprayed or greased and bake for about 24-26 minutes. (NOTE: you should have a leftover batter to make 4 more muffins, which you Store in the fridge and enjoy cold!)

Cruise Control Coffee

In this recipe you can choose between MCT or coconut oil, and between grass-fed butter

and ghee.

Servings: 1

Ingredients

1 teaspoon to 2 tablespoons of MCT oil or better still coconut oil

1 to 2 tablespoons of grass-fed, unsalted butter or better still grass-fed ghee

1 cup (about 8 to 12 ounces) of coffee

Pinch of Himalayan pink salt

Directions:

First, place all of the ingredients in a blender and blend until creamy.

Note: remember, if your mixture is really hot, I suggest, you should be careful opening up the blender before you pour. I prefer to use my Blend Tec blender because it seems to handle my coffee more safely. You can swap out coffee for tea.

If you get hungry during your evening Burn Zone hours but don't want the caffeine, I suggest you just make the recipe with any decaf beverage of your choice.

Cinnamon Spice Coffee

Servings: 1

Ingredients

1 tablespoon of MCT oil (or coconut oil)

1 tablespoon of Cruise Control (friendly sweetener)

1 cup (about 8 to 12 ounces) coffee

¼ teaspoon of ground cinnamon

Directions:

First, place all of the ingredients in a blender and blend until creamy.

Hot Coffee Cocoa

Servings: 1

Ingredients

½ cup of unsweetened almond milk

2 tablespoons of unsweetened cocoa powder

Whipped cream (it is optional)

1 cup (about 8 to 12 ounces) coffee

2 tablespoons of coconut oil (or MCT oil)

1 teaspoon of pure vanilla extract

1 tablespoon of Cruise Control (friendly sweetener)

Directions:

1. First, place the almond milk, coffee, cocoa powder, vanilla, oil, and sweetener in a blender and blend until creamy.
2. Then you top with whipped cream if desired.

Coconut Cream Latte

Servings: 1

Ingredients

2 tablespoons of unsweetened coconut milk

1 tablespoon of Cruise Control friendly sweetener

1 cup (about 8 to 12 ounces) of coffee

1 tablespoon of MCT oil (or better still coconut oil)

1 tablespoon of grass-fed, unsalted butter or better still grass-fed ghee

Directions:

First, you place all of the ingredients in a blender and blend until creamy.

Iced Caffe Mocha

Servings: 1

Ingredients

¾ cup of water

1 to 2 teaspoons of MCT oil

Ice (for serving)

2 tablespoons of freshly ground coffee beans

1 tablespoon of grass-fed unsalted butter

½ teaspoon of pure vanilla extract

1 tablespoon of Cruise Control–friendly sweetener

Directions:

1. First, you brew the coffee using pour-over, automatic machine, or French press.
2. After which you pour the freshly brewed butter, vanilla, coffee, oil, and sweetener into a blender.
3. After that, blend for a minute or until slightly frothy.
4. Finally, you serve over ice.

Iced Cruise Control Coffee

Servings: 1

Ingredients

1 teaspoon to 2 tablespoons of MCT or better still coconut oil

1 to 2 tablespoons of grass-fed, unsalted butter or better still grass-fed ghee

Ice (for serving)

1 cup (about 8 to 12 ounces) coffee

Pinch of Himalayan pink salt

1 tablespoon of Cruise Control–friendly sweetener

Directions:

1. First, place the oil, salt, coffee, butter, and sweetener in a blender and blend until smooth and creamy.
2. Then you serve over ice.
3. Tips: remember, if you have a powerful enough blender, this is super yummy with the ice; on the other hand, if blended with the other ingredients to make a Frappuccino-like drink (I use a Blend Tec).

Vanilla Cream Cold Brew

Servings: 1

Ingredients

1 teaspoon of pure vanilla extract

1 teaspoon of cinnamon + more for dusting

Whipped cream (it is optional)

8 ounces of cold brew coffee

¼ cup of heavy cream

1½ cups of unsweetened coconut milk

1 tablespoon of Cruise Control–friendly sweetener

Directions:

1. First, you place the cinnamon, cream, coffee, coconut milk, vanilla, and sweetener in a blender and blend until creamy.
2. Finally, top with whipped cream if desired and then dust with cinnamon.

Fatty Iced Matcha Tea

Servings: 1

Ingredients

1 teaspoon of grass-fed, unsalted butter or better still grass-fed ghee

1 tablespoon of Cruise Control–friendly sweetener

1 teaspoon of pure vanilla extract

1 teaspoon of matcha green tea powder

2 teaspoons of coconut oil

1 cup of ice cubes

½ cup of unsweetened coconut milk

Directions:

1. First, in a small saucepan, heat ½ cup water over medium heat.
2. After which, you make sure water does not come to a boil.
3. After that, place the matcha powder in a small bowl and pour about 1 tablespoon of the hot water on top.
4. At this point, use a spoon, stir the matcha powder into a paste.
5. Then you combine the remainder of the ghee, coconut oil, hot water, sweetener, and matcha powder in a glass.
6. Furthermore, when the tea is mixed, add 1 cup crushed ice.
7. After that, combine coconut milk and vanilla and blend.
8. Finally, you pour the mixture into the glass with the ice.

Vanilla Chai Tea Latte

Servings: 1

Ingredients

1 tablespoon of grass-fed, unsalted butter or better still grass-fed ghee

½ teaspoon of pure vanilla extract

2 tablespoons of heavy cream

2 chai tea bags

1 tablespoon of MCT oil

1 tablespoon of Cruise Control–friendly sweetener

Dash of cinnamon

Directions:

1. First, in a medium saucepan, bring 1½ cups water to a boil over medium-high heat.
2. After which you add the tea bags and brew for 10 minutes.
3. At this point, remove the tea bags.
4. Then you blend the butter, tea, oil, sweetener, vanilla, cinnamon, and cream in a blender until creamy.
5. Finally, pour into a cup and enjoy.

Butter Tea

Servings: 2

Ingredients

¼ teaspoon of salt

½ cup of heavy cream

2 tablespoons of regular or decaf loose-leaf black tea

2 tablespoons of grass-fed, unsalted butter

Directions:

1. First, in a medium saucepan, bring 2 cups water to a boil over medium high heat, then reduce the heat.
2. After which, you add the tea to the water and simmer for 2 minutes, then strain.
3. Then you cool slightly, then add the butter, salt, and cream and whisk the mixture until frothy (for 30 seconds to 1 minute).

BURN ZONE TREATS RECIPES

Cinnamon Butter Bombs

Servings: 10

Ingredients

1 cup of unsweetened coconut milk

½ teaspoon of nutmeg

1 teaspoon of Cruise Control–friendly sweetener

1 cup of coconut butter

1 teaspoon of pure vanilla extract

½ teaspoon of cinnamon

Directions:

1. Meanwhile, create a double boiler.
2. After which you place a heat-proof glass bowl over a saucepan with a few inches of water in it.
3. After that, place all of the ingredients in a double boiler over medium heat.
4. At this point, stir the ingredients as they melt.
5. Then when all the ingredients are combined, remove the bowl from the heat. (be Careful because the bowl will be hot!)
6. This is when you place the bowl in the refrigerator until the mixture solidifies.
7. Furthermore, roll the mixture into 1-inch balls.
8. In addition, you place the bombs on a platter and refrigerate for 1 hour.
9. Finally, serve and enjoy!

Strawberry Pops

Servings: 6

Ingredients

A box Simply Delish Strawberry Jel Dessert

1 cup of heavy cream

Directions:

1. First, in a small saucepan, bring ½ cup water to a boil over medium-high heat.
2. After which you remove from the heat.
3. After that, add the gelatin to the boiling water and mix until dissolved.
4. At this point, you pour the mixture into a blender and add the cream.
5. This is when you blend until smooth.
6. Then, pour into popsicle molds and freeze for 4 hours.
7. Finally, serve and enjoy!

Double Chocolate Fudge Mousse

Servings: 2

Ingredients

Simply Delish Chocolate Pudding and Pie Filling

2 cups of heavy cream

Directions:

1. First, you whisk the pudding mix with the cream in a medium bowl for 2 minutes.
2. After that, place the mixture in the refrigerator for about 10 minutes to thicken and chill.
3. Finally, pour the mousse into a glass or small bowl and enjoy!

Buttercup Gumdrops

Servings: 9

Ingredients

1 cup of coconut oil

1 tablespoon of liquid stevia

½ cup of grass-fed, unsalted butter

¼ teaspoon of sea salt

½ teaspoon of cinnamon

Directions:

1. First, you place the butter in a microwave-safe dish.
2. After which you microwave on high for 30 to 45 seconds, until melted.
3. After that, you combine the melted butter with the sea salt, oil, cinnamon, and stevia.
4. At this point, you whisk and pour into an ice cube tray.
5. This is when you place the ice cube tray in the freezer for 4 hours.
6. Finally, you remove the ice cube tray from the freezer, pop out the gumdrops, and enjoy!

Vanilla Chia Seed Pudding

Servings: 6

Ingredients

1 (14-ounce) can full-fat coconut milk

⅓ cup of Cruise Control–friendly sweetener

½ cup of chia seeds

2 teaspoons of vanilla extract

Directions:

1. First, you mix the chia seeds with 1½ cups hot water in a large bowl.
2. After which you add vanilla, coconut milk, and sweetener and mix with a spoon.
3. Finally, you separate equally into 6 cups or bowls of your choice and refrigerate for 1 hour or overnight.

Peppermint Fat Bombs

Servings: 6

Ingredients

1 tablespoon of Cruise Control–friendly sweetener

2 tablespoons of unsweetened cocoa powder

10 tablespoons of coconut oil (melted)

1 teaspoon of peppermint extract

Directions:

1. First, combine the coconut oil with the sweetener and peppermint extract in a small bowl.
2. After which you pour half of the mixture into ice cube trays.
3. At this point, place in the fridge (NOTE: This will become the
4. white layer).
5. This is when you add cocoa powder to the remaining mixture, then pour on top of the white layer.
6. Then you place back into the refrigerator until set completely, then freeze for 2 to 3 hours.
7. Finally, serve and enjoy!

BOOST ZONE MEALS

Savory Italian Egg Bake

Ingredients:

3 tablespoons of mustard

½ cup of heavy whipping cream

2 cups of diced cooked chicken breast

½ cup of grated Parmesan cheese

1 cup of shredded extra sharp cheese

10 large eggs

2 teaspoons of garlic and herb seasoning

½ cup of tomato sauce

12 ounces of frozen broccoli florets

1 teaspoon of parsley flakes

Directions:

1. Meanwhile, you heat oven to 350°F. In a large mixing bowl, whisk together the eggs.
2. After which you whisk in the mustard, garlic and herb seasoning, and heavy whipping cream.
3. Then, when that's blended well, slowly whisk in the tomato sauce until it's no longer lumpy.
4. After that, you add in the diced chicken and broccoli florets.
5. At this point, you grease a casserole dish or a large baking pan then pour in the Italian bake.
6. This is when you sprinkle Parmesan cheese and parsley flakes on top of the Italian bake.

7. Then you bake for about 30-40 minutes at 350°F, or until the top looks like a crust.
8. Remember, before serving, I want you to top the Italian bake with some sharp extra sharp cheese. NOTE: You could also use any other cheese of your choosing, such as mozzarella or pepper jack.

Sausage and Kale Soup

Ingredients:

1 Tablespoon of butter

1 medium carrot (peeled and diced)

2 tablespoons of red wine vinegar

1 teaspoon of dried basil

¼ to ½ teaspoon of crushed red pepper flakes

1 cup of heavy cream

3 cups of kale (chopped)

½ teaspoon of freshly ground black pepper

1 lb. of ground sweet Italian sausage

1 medium yellow onion (chopped)

2 cloves garlic (crushed)

1 teaspoon of dried oregano

1 teaspoon of dried rubbed sage

4 cups of low-sodium chicken broth

½ medium head cauliflower (cut into small florets)

½ to 1 teaspoon of sea salt (or to taste)

Directions:

1. First, you heat a large saucepan or Dutch oven over medium high heat.
2. After which you add ground sausage, breaking up the meat.
3. After that, you cook, stirring occasionally until browned and cooked through about 5 minutes.
4. Then you use a slotted spoon, to remove cooked sausage and allow to drain on a plate covered with paper towels.
5. Furthermore, you discard drippings, but do not wash pan.
6. After which you melt butter over medium heat.

7. Then, when bubbling subsides, add onion and carrot.
8. After that, you cook until onion begins to brown on the edges and becomes somewhat translucent.
9. This is when you stir garlic into onion and carrot mixture.
10. Cook one minute and add red wine vinegar and cook until syrupy, scraping up browned bits-about 1 minute.
11. At this point, you stir in oregano, basil, sage and red pepper flakes.
12. After that, you pour in the stock and heavy cream. Increase heat to medium high.
13. Then, when soup reaches a simmer, add cauliflower and turn heat down to medium-low.
14. Then you simmer uncovered until cauliflower is fork-tender, about 10 minutes.
15. Stir in kale and cooked sausage; cook 1 to 2 minutes longer, or until kale wilts and the sausage is reheated.
16. Finally, you season to taste with salt and pepper. (NOTE: the amount of salt needed may vary due to variation in brands of broth.)

Broccoli Chicken Zucchini Boats

Nutritional value:

Note: this makes a total of 2 servings of Broccoli Chicken Zucchini Boats.

Ingredients:

2 tablespoons of Butter

1 cup of Broccoli

2 tablespoons of Sour Cream

Salt and Pepper (to taste)

10 oz. Zucchini (2 large zucchinis, hollowed out)

3 oz. Cheddar Cheese (shredded)

6 oz. Rotisserie Chicken (shredded)

1 stalk of Green Onion

Directions:

1. Meanwhile, you heat the oven to 400F and cut the zucchini you're using in half lengthwise.
2. After which you use a spoon, scoop out most of the zucchini until you're left with a shell about ½ - 1 cm thick.
3. After that, you pour 1 tablespoon of melted butter into each zucchini boat, season with salt/pepper and place them in the oven for about 20 minutes.
4. Then, while zucchini is cooking, shred your rotisserie chicken and measure out 6 oz.
5. At this point, you cut up broccoli florets into small pieces, and combine both with sour cream.
6. This is when you season with salt and pepper.
7. Then, once the zucchini is done, take them out and add your chicken and broccoli filling.
8. Furthermore, you sprinkle cheddar cheese and bake for an additional 10-15 minutes or until the cheese is melted and browning.
9. Finally, you garnish with chopped green onion and enjoy with more sour cream or mayo!

Mug Lasagna

Note: this makes a total of 1servings of Mug Lasagna.

Ingredients:

3 tablespoons of Rao's marinara

3 ounces of whole milk mozzarella

1/3 (about 65 g) zucchini

2 tablespoons of whole milk ricotta

Directions:

1. First, you slice the zucchini into paper thin rounds. (NOTE: feel free to use a really sharp knife or a mandolin.)
2. After which, in the bottom of your dish add a tablespoon of the marinara.
3. After that, you layer on some of the zucchini.
4. Then you carefully spread out 1 tablespoon of ricotta.
5. This is when you add another tablespoon of marinara.
6. At this point, you layer on the second layer of zucchini, another tablespoon of ricotta, any leftover zucchini, and then the last tablespoon of marinara.
7. After that, you top with the mozzarella.
8. Finally, you microwave for about 3-4 minutes, depending on the strength of your microwave.
9. Remember that you can always sprinkle on a little oregano or Parmesan cheese if you like.

Salmon Patties with Fresh Herbs

Note: this makes a total of 5 servings of Salmon Patties with Fresh Herbs.

Ingredients:

2 tablespoons of chopped fresh chives

¼ cup of grated Parmesan cheese

2 large eggs

Salt and pepper (to taste)

2 tablespoons of olive oil

2 (about 14.75-oz) cans pink salmon

¼ cup of chopped fresh dill

4 ounces' pork rinds (crushed)

1 teaspoon of lemon zest

½ cup of almond flour

Directions:

1. First, you open and drain both cans of pink salmon and then add to a large mixing bowl.
2. After which you mix the Parmesan cheese, crushed pork rinds, chives, dill, 2 large eggs, lemon zest, and the salt and pepper into the salmon.
3. After that, you form the salmon into 3 ounce balls. (NOTE: I usually end up with about 10.)
4. Then you put the almond flour in a plate. (NOTE: Carefully flatten each salmon patty in the palm of your hand and then dip into the almond flour.)
5. Remember, they are fragile so I prefer to place the patty into the flour and then scoop some of the flour on top of the salmon, and then lightly tap it down with my fingers.
6. Meanwhile, you heat a skillet with 2 tablespoons of olive oil.
7. After that, you fry the patties over medium-high heat for a few minutes on each side. Note that they should be cooked through and browned when finished.
8. Finally, you serve two patties with some of our homemade tartar sauce, and veggies.

Zucchini “Linguine” Shakshuka

Servings: 1

Ingredients

½ onion (diced)

½ red bell pepper (diced)

2 tablespoons of tomato paste

2 large eggs

Salt and freshly ground pepper to taste (it is optional)

1 tablespoon of extra-virgin olive oil

1 clove garlic (crushed)

1 can of fire-roasted diced tomatoes

2 cups of zucchini in spiralized linguine-shaped noodles

1 avocado (sliced)

Note: I prefer to use a pack of Cece’s Veggie Co. organic zucchini veggiccine.

Directions:

1. Meanwhile, heat the oven to 350°F.
2. After which you heat oil in a cast-iron skillet for about 3 to 4 minutes over medium-high heat.
3. After that, add the garlic, onion, and bell pepper and sauté for about 3 minutes until starting to soften.
4. Then drain a third of the liquid from the tomatoes and add the rest to the skillet with the tomato paste.
5. At this point, simmer for about 2 to 3 more minutes.
6. Furthermore, saving a small handful for garnish, stir in zucchini linguine and continue to cook for 3 more minutes.
7. After which you remove the skillet from the heat.
8. Then, you push the ingredients with a spoon to create two craters and crack the eggs into them.
9. This is when you place the skillet in the preheated oven.

10. In addition, bake for 15 minutes or until the eggs are set.
11. At this point, remove from the oven and top with avocado slices and raw zucchini linguine noodles.
12. Finally, season with salt and pepper if desired.

Dr. Weil's Tuscan Kale Salad

Servings: 1

Ingredients

Juice of 1 lemon

2 cloves garlic (mashed)

Hot red pepper flakes (to taste)

½ cup of freshly made breadcrumbs from lightly toasted bread

4 to 6 cups of loosely packed, bite-size sliced leaves of Italian black kale, thick ribs removed

3 to 4 tablespoons of extra-virgin olive oil

Salt and freshly ground pepper (to taste)

⅔ cup of grated Pecorino Toscano cheese or better still any other grated Italian cheese

Directions:

1. **First, p**lace the kale in a serving bowl.
2. **After which you w**hisk together the olive oil, lemon juice, salt, garlic, black pepper, and a generous pinch of red pepper flakes.
3. **After that, p**our the dressing over the kale and toss well.
4. Then add the cheese, reserving 2 tablespoons, and toss again.
5. **At this point, l**et the kale sit for at least 5 minutes.
6. **Finally, a**dd the breadcrumbs, toss again, and top with the remaining cheese.

Mug Omelet

If I come back home starving, I'll often throw this super simple "omelet" together it so cool.

Servings: 1

Ingredients

½ bell pepper (diced)

Salt and freshly ground black pepper (to taste)

2 large eggs

2 slices ham (diced)

¼ cup of fresh spinach

Directions:

1. First, you combine all of the ingredients in a microwavable mug.
2. After which you cook for 2 to 3 minutes, making sure the egg doesn't bubble over.
3. After that, stir halfway through the cooking process.
4. Then you enjoy!

One-Pan Italian Sausage & Veggies

Servings: 6

Ingredients

2 cups of red potato

2 cups of red bell pepper

16 ounces smoked Italian turkey (or better still chicken sausage)

1½ teaspoons of dried oregano

1½ teaspoons of garlic powder

½ teaspoon thyme (dried)

⅛ teaspoon of freshly ground black pepper (it is optional)

⅛ teaspoon crushed red pepper flakes (it is optional)

Fresh parsley (optional)

2 cups of carrot

2⅓ cups of zucchini

1½ cups of broccoli

1½ teaspoons of dried basil

1½ teaspoons of dried parsley

½ teaspoon of onion powder

½ teaspoon of salt (if desired)

4½ tablespoons of extra-virgin olive oil

⅓ cup of freshly grated Parmesan cheese (it is optional)

Directions:

1. Meanwhile, heat the oven to 400°F.
2. After which you line a large rimmed baking sheet with parchment paper or foil.
3. After that, peel and thinly slice the carrots.

4. At this point, wash and chop the potatoes in half, then cut each half into 10 to 12 pieces.
5. Then you cut the zucchini in half and cut each side into thick coins (NOTE: Coarsely chop the broccoli).
6. Furthermore, remove the stems and seeds from the bell peppers and chop into medium-size pieces.
7. After which you chop the sausage into thick coins.
8. Then you arrange the veggies and sausage on the prepared baking sheet.
9. In addition, combine the oregano, garlic powder, crushed red pepper flakes, basil, parsley, onion powder, thyme, and salt and pepper if desired with the olive oil in a small bowl; stir to combine.
10. After that, pour the seasoning-and-oil mixture on top of the veggies and sausage and toss to coat.
11. This is when you place in the oven and cook for 15 minutes.
12. At this point, remove from the oven, toss the veggies and sausage, and return to the oven for another 10 to 20 minutes or until the vegetables are crisp-tender.
13. Then, you top with freshly grated Parmesan cheese and parsley if desired.
14. Finally, serve and enjoy!

One-Pot Shrimp Alfredo

Servings: 4

Ingredients:

1-pound of raw shrimp

½ cup of whole milk

1 teaspoon of dried basil

½ cup of shredded Parmesan cheese

¼ cup of baby kale (or spinach)

1 tablespoon of grass-fed salted butter

4 ounces of cream cheese (cubed)

1 tablespoon of garlic powder

1 teaspoon of salt

5 whole sun-dried tomatoes (cut into strips)

Directions:

1. First, melt the butter in a large skillet over medium heat.
2. After which you add the shrimp to the skillet and reduce the heat to medium-low.
3. After that, turn shrimp after 30 seconds and cook the other side until slightly pink. (NOTE: This is important because the sauce will continue to cook the shrimp once it is added. Reason: if you overcook the shrimp, it will become tough and rubbery!)
4. Then add the cream cheese cubes and milk to the pan and reduce the heat to medium.
5. At this point, stir frequently until the cream cheese has melted into the milk and there are no lumps.
6. This is when you sprinkle with the basil, garlic powder, and salt and stir well.
7. Furthermore, add the Parmesan and stir to combine.

8. After that, let simmer until the sauce begins to thicken.
9. Then you complete the dish by folding in the sun-dried tomatoes and baby kale.
10. Finally, remove from the heat and serve.

Bruschetta Burgers

Servings: 4

Ingredients:

¼ cup of grated Parmesan cheese

1 teaspoon of onion powder

½ tablespoon of balsamic vinegar

Freshly ground black pepper

5 thick slices of fresh mozzarella

Balsamic glaze (for drizzling)

1 pound of ground chicken

2 cloves of garlic

2 tablespoons of torn basil leave (plus more for garnish)

Kosher salt

1 tablespoon of extra-virgin olive oil

8 slices tomato

1 cup of baby spinach

Directions:

1. First, in a large bowl, combine the ground chicken, garlic, onion powder, Parmesan, basil, and vinegar.
2. After which you season with salt and pepper, then form the mixture into 4 small patties, depending on the size of your tomatoes. (NOTE: They should be approximately the same size!)
3. After that, in a large skillet, heat the olive oil over medium heat.
4. Then you add the patties and turn after 6 minutes and seared on one side.
5. At this point, flip again for about 4 minutes, then top with the mozzarella.
6. This is when you cover the skillet and cook for 2 to 3 more minutes, until the cheese melts and the chicken is cooked through.
7. Furthermore, slice the tomatoes in half.

8. After that, season the bottom tomato halves with salt and pepper.
9. In addition, top with the baby spinach, the burgers, and the basil garnish, then drizzle with the balsamic glaze.
10. Finally, you top with the remaining tomato halves.

Taco-Stuffed Avocados

Servings: 6

Ingredients:

1 tablespoon of chili powder

¾ teaspoon of cumin

¼ teaspoon of garlic powder

4 ounces of tomato sauce

1 cup of shredded Cheddar cheese

¼ cup lettuce (shredded)

⅓ cup of cilantro (chopped)

1 pound of ground beef

½ teaspoon of salt

½ teaspoon of dried oregano

¼ teaspoon of onion powder

3 avocados (halved)

¼ cup of cherry tomatoes (sliced)

6 tablespoons of sour cream

Directions:

1. First, add the ground beef to a medium saucepan.
2. After which you cook over medium heat until browned.
3. After that, drain the grease and add the salt, chili powder, cumin, garlic powder, oregano, onion powder, and tomato sauce.
4. Then you stir to combine and cook for about 3 to 4 minutes.
5. At this point, remove the pits from halved avocados and fill with the taco meat.
6. This is when you top each "taco" with tomatoes, cheese, one tablespoon of sour cream, and a sprinkling of cilantro.
7. Finally, serve and enjoy!

Portobello Mini Pizzas

Tip: this is a Cruiser favorite.

Servings: 2

Ingredients:

½ cup of pesto

10 black Kalamata olives

Pinch of crushed red pepper flakes and basil for garnish (it is optional)

2 large Portobello caps (with stems removed)

1 cup of shredded Italian blend cheese

1 tablespoon of capers

Directions:

1. Meanwhile, heat the oven to 375°F.
2. After which you place the mushrooms on a rimmed baking sheet.
3. After that, spread ¼ cup pesto in each mushroom cap.
4. Then fill the centers with cheese, then top with olives and capers.
5. At this point, bake for 10 to 15 minutes or just until the cheese is bubbly and mushrooms are starting to soften.
6. Finally, sprinkle with red pepper flakes and basil, if using, or refrigerate for up to a day and reheat before serving.

My Big Fat Greek Salad

Servings: 2

Salad

1 tablespoon of extra-virgin olive oil

1 garlic clove (crushed)

2 cups of romaine lettuce (chopped)

1 cup of cherry or grape tomatoes (cut in half)

1 (6.5-ounce) jar diced marinated artichoke hearts

¼ cup of pitted Kalamata olives

2 medium skinless, boneless chicken breasts, pounded flat

1½ teaspoons of dried oregano

Salt and freshly ground pepper (to taste)

1 avocado (peeled, pitted, and chopped)

½ red onion (sliced thinly)

¼ cup of feta cheese

Dressing

2 tablespoons of raw apple cider vinegar

1 small garlic clove (minced)

½ teaspoon of dried oregano

½ teaspoon of freshly ground black pepper

¼ cup of extra-virgin olive oil

Juice of ½ lemon

½ teaspoon of Dijon mustard

½ teaspoon of salt

Directions:

1. First, pound the chicken flat with a meat tenderizer or slice the chicken breasts in half to make thinner.
2. After which in a medium bowl or Ziploc bag, combine the chicken, olive oil, garlic, oregano, salt, and pepper.
3. After that, heat a large, heavy-duty pan over medium heat and cook each side of chicken for 5 to 6 minutes or until tender and cooked through.
4. Then remove the chicken from the pan, cool for 5 minutes, then slice or chop.
5. At this point, combine all of the ingredients for the dressing in a small bowl and whisk.
6. In addition, in a large bowl, combine the avocado, lettuce, tomatoes, onion, feta, artichoke hearts, and olives.
7. Finally, top with chicken and drizzle the dressing generously.

No-Cook Bento Box

Servings: 1

Ingredients:

1 teaspoon of ranch seasoning

½ small cucumber (sliced)

¼ cup of blackberries

¼ cup of hazelnuts

2 tablespoons of cream cheese

3 slices deli turkey (with no added sugar)

½ red bell pepper (sliced)

¼ cup of Colby Jack cheese (or better still Cheddar cheese, cubed)

Directions:

1. **First, i**n a small bowl, mix the cream cheese and ranch seasoning until smooth.
2. After which you smear the cream cheese mixture on the turkey slices.
3. After that, top with a slice of cucumber and bell pepper, and then roll up in the turkey and cut in half.
4. **Then, p**lace the turkey roll-ups in the container with the cheese, blackberries, and nuts.
5. Enjoy!

Egg Drop Soup

Servings: 6

Ingredients:

1 tablespoon of freshly grated turmeric (or better still 1 teaspoon ground turmeric)

2 cloves garlic (minced)

2 cups of sliced brown mushrooms

4 cups of chopped Swiss chard leaves or spinach

2 medium spring onions (sliced)

6 tablespoons of extra-virgin olive oil

2 quarts' chicken or bone broth (Kettle and Fire)

1 tablespoon of freshly grated ginger (or better still 1 teaspoon ground ginger)

1 small chili pepper (sliced)

2 tablespoons of coconut aminos (or soy sauce)

4 large eggs

2 tablespoons of freshly chopped cilantro

1 teaspoon of salt or to taste

Directions:

1. **First, p**our the chicken stock in a large pot and place over medium heat, until it starts to simmer.
2. **After which you a**dd the ginger, turmeric, chili pepper, garlic, mushrooms, and coconut aminos to the stock and simmer for 5 minutes.
3. **After that, a**dd the chard leaves and cook for 1 minute.
4. Then, in a separate bowl, whisk the eggs and slowly pour them into the simmering soup.
5. **At this point, k**eep stirring until the eggs are cooked, then remove the pot from the heat.
6. This is when you add the onions and cilantro to the soup and season with salt and pepper.

7. Finally, pour into a serving bowl and drizzle with the olive oil.
8. Make sure you eat immediately or let it cool down and store in an airtight container for up to 5 days.

BLT Ranch Wrap

Servings: 1

Ingredients for Ranch Dressing

1 teaspoon of lemon juice

¼ teaspoon of garlic powder

Pinch of sea salt and freshly ground black pepper

3 to 4 leaves leaf lettuce

¼ small avocado (sliced)

1 tablespoon of mayonnaise

1 teaspoon of dried parsley

¼ teaspoon of onion powder

Lettuce Wrap

2 slices of cooked bacon

2 to 3 tomatoes (sliced)

Directions:

1. First, mix the ranch ingredients together in a small bowl.
2. After which you arrange the lettuce in a single layer slightly overlapping.
3. After that, drizzle with ranch dressing.
4. Then top with bacon, tomato, and avocado.
5. Finally, roll the lettuce like a sushi roll and tuck the edges as you go; once wrapped, cut in half.
6. Enjoy!

Zoodle Spaghetti & Meatballs

This recipe is a great one for kids.

Servings: 6

Ingredients for Meatballs

½ pound of ground turkey

1 teaspoon of Italian seasoning

¼ onion (minced)

2 large eggs

2 tablespoons of gluten-free breadcrumbs

Extra-virgin olive oil

¾ pound of ground beef

¼ cup of grated Parmesan cheese

Salt and freshly ground black pepper (to taste)

2 garlic cloves (minced)

¼ cup of whole milk

2 tablespoons of chopped fresh parsley

Ingredients for Sauce and Zoodles

5 to 6 medium zucchini (about 2¼ pounds total)

4-5 tablespoons of extra-virgin olive oil

1 medium onion (finely chopped)

2 carrots (peeled and diced)

3 cloves garlic (finely chopped)

3 tablespoons of tomato paste

1 (14.5-ounce) can diced tomatoes

1 (14.5-ounce) can crushed tomatoes

1 cup of low-sodium beef broth

1 teaspoon of dried oregano

1 bay leaf

¾ teaspoon of dried basil

Chopped fresh parsley (for serving)

Grated Parmesan cheese (for serving)

Directions for the meatballs:

1. First, you combine turkey, ground beef, cheese, salt, Italian seasoning, pepper, onion, and garlic together.
2. After which you mix in milk, eggs, breadcrumbs, and parsley until just combined.
3. Then, form meatballs and cook in 2 to 3 tablespoons of oil over medium heat for 8 to 10 minutes.

Directions for the sauce:

1. First, you heat 1 tablespoon olive oil in a wide, deep skillet on medium-high heat and add onion and carrots.
2. After which you sauté for 2 to 3 minutes.
3. After that, add garlic and tomato paste and mix in onion, carrot mixture.
4. At this point, add both cans of tomatoes, oregano, the broth, bay leaf, and basil.
5. Finally, cover and turn heat to low.
6. Then, you simmer for 20 to 30 minutes, stirring occasionally.

Directions for the zoodles:

1. First, you spiralize the zucchini into zucchini noodles using a spiralizer or vegetable peeler.
2. After which you add the olive oil to a pan and cook the zoodles over medium heat for 1 to 2 minutes or until slightly softened and beginning to brown.
3. After that, transfer the zoodles and meatballs to a serving bowl.
4. Finally, add the sauce and sprinkling of freshly chopped parsley and Parmesan cheese.

Nacho Steak Skillet

Servings: 6

Ingredients:

⅓ cup of coconut oil

½ teaspoon of turmeric

8 ounces' beef. (NOTE: Any boneless cut steak on the thinner side will do, such as strip, ribeye, or flat iron)

¼ cup of shredded Cheddar cheese

⅛ cup of canned jalapeño slices

½ teaspoon of hot sauce

1½ pounds of cauliflower

1 teaspoon of chili powder

Salt and freshly ground black pepper (to taste)

1 tablespoon of butter

¼ cup of shredded Monterey Jack cheese

⅓ cup of sour cream

1 avocado

Directions:

1. **Meanwhile,** heat the oven to 400°F.
2. After which you remove the leaves and bottom of the stem from the
3. cauliflower.
4. After that, slice the cauliflower across the head.
5. Then, in a large bowl combine the chili powder, coconut oil, and turmeric.
6. At this point, add the cauliflower and toss until it's evenly coated.
7. This is when you spread the cauliflower out on a rimmed baking sheet.
8. In addition, season with salt and pepper.

9. After that, roast for 20 to 25 minutes, until it has softened and the edges are golden brown.
10. Meanwhile, heat a cast-iron skillet over medium-high heat.
11. After which you season both sides of the steak with salt and pepper.
12. Then you melt the butter in the skillet; add the steak.
13. Furthermore, cook through, about 3 minutes, then flip to cook the other side for 3 more minutes.
14. Remove the steak from the pan; allow the steak to rest for about 5 to 10 minutes.
15. Then, once the cauliflower is done, remove it from the oven and transfer the florets to the cast-iron skillet.
16. This is when you slice up the steak into strips.
17. Top the cauliflower with the steak; then top with both shredded cheeses and the jalapeño slices.
18. At this point, place the skillet in the oven and bake for another 5 to 10 minutes, until the cheese has melted.
19. Finally, peel and de-pit the avocado and mash it in a small bowl with the hot sauce.
20. You can serve with guacamole, sour cream, and hot sauce.

Cashew Chicken

Servings: 3

Ingredients

3 skinless, boneless chicken thighs

¼ medium white onion

1 tablespoon of green onions

1½ teaspoons of chili garlic sauce

Salt and freshly ground black pepper (to taste)

1 teaspoon of sesame seeds

¼ cup of raw cashews

½ medium green bell pepper

2 tablespoons of coconut oil

1 tablespoon of minced garlic

½ teaspoon of ground ginger

1 tablespoon of rice wine vinegar

1 tablespoon of sesame oil

Directions:

1. First, heat a medium pan over low heat and toast the cashews for 8 minutes.
2. After which you remove and set aside.
3. After that, dice the chicken thighs into chunks.
4. Then, cut the bell pepper and white onion into large chunks.
5. At this point, raise the heat to high and add the coconut oil to the pan.
6. This is when you add the chicken and cook for 5 minutes.
7. Furthermore, add the white onions, bell pepper, green onions, chili garlic sauce, garlic, ginger, salt, and black pepper.
8. After that, cook for 2 to 3 minutes.
9. In addition, add the rice wine vinegar and cashews.
10. Then you cook for 2 to 3 more minutes.

11. Finally, you serve in a bowl (NOTE: Top with sesame seeds and drizzle with sesame oil).
12. Enjoy!

Ham & Goat Cheese Frittata

Servings: 6

Ingredients:

¼ onion (diced)

⅓ cup of chopped broccoli florets

8 large eggs

6 ounces of chopped smoked ham

4 ounces of goat cheese

1 tablespoon of extra-virgin olive oil

½ pound asparagus, ends trimmed and cut into approximately 2-inch pieces

½ red bell pepper (chopped)

¼ cup of heavy cream

½ teaspoon of garlic powder

½ cup of grated Cheddar cheese

Directions:

1. Meanwhile, heat the oven to 400°F.
2. After which in an oven-proof non-stick skillet over medium heat, heat the olive oil and add the asparagus, onion, broccoli, and bell pepper.
3. After that, cook for 2 to 3 minutes.
4. Then you whisk eggs with the cream and ham.
5. At this point, stir in the garlic powder and Cheddar cheese.
6. This is when you pour the eggs into the same pan with the asparagus, and top with crumbled goat cheese.
7. Furthermore, transfer the pan to the oven and cook for 15 minutes.
8. Finally, cut into wedges and serve!

Broccoli Cheese Soup

Servings: 8

Ingredients:

1 stalk celery (chopped)

1½ pounds of broccoli florets (chopped)

1 teaspoon of garlic powder

Salt and freshly ground black pepper (to taste)

1 pouch of Parmesan crisps (Parm Crisps)

2 tablespoons of grass-fed salted butter

1 onion (chopped)

3 cups of chicken broth (or better still bone broth)

1 teaspoon of paprika

3 cups of Cheddar cheese (grated)

Directions:

1. First, in a stockpot, melt the butter over medium heat.
2. After which you cook the celery and onion in the butter until softened, about 3 minutes.
3. After that, stir in the broccoli, then cover with the stock; simmer for 10 minutes.
4. At this point, reduce the heat and stir in the garlic powder and paprika and salt and pepper if desired.
5. This is when you add the Cheddar cheese gradually and continue to stir until melted.
6. Then top with Parm Crisps; serve and enjoy.

5-Minute Tuna Salad

Servings: 2

Ingredients

1 tablespoon of lemon juice

1 tablespoon of chopped parsley

¼ teaspoon of freshly ground black pepper

1 medium cucumber (sliced)

1 (5-ounce) can tuna (drained)

4 large hard-boiled eggs

¼ cup of mayonnaise

2 tablespoons of extra-virgin olive oil

¼ teaspoon of salt

1 head romaine lettuce

½ small onion (sliced)

8 large olives (sliced)

Directions:

1. **First, p**lace the lemon juice, mayonnaise, olive oil, salt, parsley, and pepper in a small bowl and whisk until blended.
2. **After which you s**eparate the lettuce leaves and fold them into a medium bowl.
3. **After that, a**dd the onion, cucumber, tuna, and olives on top of the lettuce leaves.
4. **Then s**lice the eggs into quarters and add to salad.
5. **At this point, d**rizzle the dressing onto the salad.
6. Finally, serve and enjoy!

Sheet Pan Salmon & Asparagus

Servings: 4

Ingredients:

2 tablespoons of mayonnaise

¼ cup of grated Parmesan cheese

1 tablespoon of extra-virgin olive oil

½ teaspoon of kosher salt

2 tablespoons of chopped parsley (for garnish)

1 pound wild-caught salmon fillets

1 teaspoon of Dijon mustard

1 pound of fresh asparagus (ends trimmed)

2 lemons

¼ teaspoon of ground black pepper

Directions:

1. Meanwhile, heat the oven to 325°F.
2. After which you rinse and pat dry the salmon fillets; remove any bones.
3. After that, mix together the mayonnaise and mustard in a small bowl.
4. Then brush the mayonnaise mixture over the top of the salmon.
5. At this point, sprinkle the Parmesan on top.
6. This is when you place the asparagus on a rimmed baking sheet and drizzle with olive oil.
7. Furthermore, spread the asparagus out on the baking sheet, leaving room in the centre for the salmon.
8. After that, place the salmon on the baking sheet.
9. In addition, cut the lemons in half and place them, cut-side up, on the baking sheet.
10. After which you sprinkle the entire pan with salt and pepper; bake for 18 minutes.
11. Finally, remove from the oven and squeeze lemon juice over the asparagus and salmon, removing any lemon seeds.

12. You can garnish with parsley and serve warm.

Cauliflower Pepperoni Pizza

Servings: 2

Crust

Ingredients

1 large egg

⅓ cup of grated Parmesan cheese

1 teaspoon of dried oregano

Extra-virgin olive oil

1½ cup of cauliflower rice

½ cup of grated mozzarella cheese

1 teaspoon of dried basil

½ teaspoon of garlic powder

½ teaspoon of salt

Sauce

1 tablespoon of fresh basil

2 tablespoons of extra-virgin olive oil

1 tablespoon of fresh parsley

1 clove garlic (minced)

1 tablespoon of tomato puree

½ teaspoon of dried fennel seeds

Toppings

10 slices pepperoni ham

¼ cup of grated Parmesan cheese

¼ cup of grated mozzarella cheese

¼ cup of chopped fresh basil leaves

Directions:

1. Meanwhile, heat the oven to 450°F.
2. After which in a large bowl, mix the cauliflower rice with the egg, Parmesan, garlic powder, mozzarella, basil, oregano, and salt.
3. After that, line a baking sheet with a non-stick spray or parchment paper.
4. Then press the cauliflower mixture evenly on the pan.
5. At this point, spray with some extra-virgin olive oil.
6. This is when you bake for 15 to 20 minutes, until the mixture begins to turn golden brown.
7. Furthermore, remove the baking sheet from the oven and set aside.

Direction for the pizza sauce:

1. First, mash the garlic and chop the basil.
2. After which you place them in a small bowl and add the tomato puree, fennel seeds, olive oil, and parsley; mix with a spoon.
3. After that, spread the sauce evenly over the pizza crust.
4. Then top with grated mozzarella, basil, pepperoni ham, and Parmesan.
5. Finally, place in the oven and cook for an additional 10 minutes.
6. enjoy!

BOOST ZONE SNACKS

Cheesy Cauliflower Onion Dip

Ingredients:

1 ½ cups of chicken broth

¼ cup of mayonnaise

½ teaspoon of ground cumin

½ teaspoon of garlic powder

½ teaspoon of salt

1 pound or 1 large head cauliflower

½ cup of medium-sized onion

¾ cup of cream cheese

½ teaspoon of chili powder

½ teaspoon of ground black pepper

Directions:

1. First, you simmer the cauliflower and half an onion in chicken broth until soft and tender.
2. After which you stir in the cumin, garlic powder, chili powder, pepper, and salt.
3. After that, you cut up chunks of cream cheese, and whisk into the cauliflower until the cream cheese melts and is no longer chunky.
4. Then you use a stick blender, or a regular blender, to blend the mixture until it's smooth.
5. At this point, you carefully whisk in the mayonnaise.
6. Finally, you chill in the fridge 2-3 hours before serving.

Pesto Crackers

Ingredients:

¼ teaspoon of ground black pepper

½ teaspoon of baking powder

Pinch of cayenne pepper

3 Tablespoons of butter

1 ¼ cups of almond flour

½ teaspoon of salt

¼ teaspoon of dried basil

1 clove of garlic (pressed)

2 Tablespoons of basil pesto

Directions:

1. Meanwhile, you heat oven to 325 degrees Fahrenheit.
2. After which you line a cookie sheet with parchment paper.
3. Then, in a medium bowl, combine almond flour, pepper, salt and baking powder and whisk until smooth.
4. After that, you add basil, cayenne, and garlic and stir until evenly combined.
5. Then add in the pesto and whisk until the dough forms into coarse crumbs.
6. At this point, you cut the butter into the cracker mixture with a fork or your fingers until the dough forms into a ball.
7. This is when you transfer the dough onto the prepared cookie sheet and spread out the dough thinly until it's about 1 ½ mm thick. (NOTE: Make sure the thickness is the same throughout so that the crackers bake evenly.)
8. Furthermore, you place the pan in the preheated oven and bake for 14-17 minutes until light golden brown in colour.
9. Once the dough has finished baking, I suggest is time to remove it from the oven.
10. Finally, you cut into crackers of the desired size or break into pieces.

Neopolitan Fat Bombs

Note: this makes a total of 24 Neapolitan Fat Bombs.

Ingredients:

½ of cup Coconut Oil

½ cup of Cream Cheese

2 tablespoons of Erythritol

1 teaspoon of Vanilla Extract

½ cup of Butter

½ cup of Sour Cream

2 tablespoons of Cocoa Powder

25 drops of Liquid Stevia

2 medium Strawberries

Directions:

1. First, you combine all ingredients (except for cocoa powder, vanilla, and strawberries) in a bowl.
2. After which you use an immersion blender to mix it together.
3. After that, you separate the mixture between 3 bowls.
4. Then you add cocoa powder to one, vanilla to another, and strawberries to the last.
5. At this point, you pour chocolate mixture into fat bomb mold, then freeze for 30 minutes. (NOTE: repeat with vanilla and strawberry layers.)
6. Finally, you let freeze for at least 1 hour.

Coconut Orange Creamsicle Fat Bombs

Note: this makes a total of 10 Coconut Orange Creamsicle Fat Bombs.

Ingredients:

½ cup of Heavy Whipping Cream

10 drops of Liquid Stevia

½ cup of coconut oil

4 oz. of Cream Cheese

1 tsp. of Orange Vanilla Mio

Directions:

1. First, you use an immersion blender to blend together all of the ingredients. (NOTE: If you're having a hard time blending the ingredients, you can microwave them to soften them up.)
2. After which you spread the mixture into a silicone tray and freeze for 2-3 hours.
3. Then, once hardened, remove from the silicone tray and store in the freezer.

Savory Pizza Fat Bombs

Note: this makes a total of 6 Pizza Fat Bombs.

Ingredients:

14 slices Pepperoni

2 tablespoons of Sun Dried Tomato Pesto

Salt and Pepper (to Taste)

4 oz. of Cream Cheese

8 pitted Black Olives

2 tablespoons of Fresh Basil (chopped)

Directions:

1. First, you dice pepperoni and olives into small pieces.
2. After which you mix together all of the ingredients.
3. Then, you form into balls, then garnish with pepperoni, basil, and olive.

No Bake Chocolate Peanut Butter Fat Bombs

Note: this makes a total of 8 No Bake Chocolate Peanut Butter Fat Bombs.

Ingredients:

¼ cup of cocoa powder

6 tablespoons of Shelled Hemp Seeds

1 teaspoon of Vanilla Extract

¼ cup of Unsweetened Shredded Coconut

½ cup of Coconut Oil

4 tablespoons of PB Fit Powder

2 tablespoons of Heavy Cream

28 drops of Liquid Stevia

Directions:

1. First, you mix together all of the dry ingredients with the coconut oil. (NOTE: it may take a bit of work, but it will eventually turn into a paste.)
2. After which you add heavy cream, vanilla, and liquid stevia.
3. After that, you mix again until everything is combined and slightly creamy.
4. Then you measure out unsweetened shredded coconut on to a plate.
5. At this point, you roll balls out using your hand and then roll in the unsweetened shredded coconut.
6. Finally, you lay on to a baking tray covered with parchment paper.
7. Then you set in the freezer for about 20 minutes.

Smoked Salmon and Goat Cheese Bites

Note: this makes a total of 16 servings of Smoked Salmon & Goat Cheese Bites.

Ingredients:

1 tablespoon (about 2 g) fresh oregano

1 tablespoon (about 2.65 g) fresh basil

Salt and pepper (to taste)

4 ounces (about 113.4 g) smoked salmon

8 ounces (about 228 g) goat cheese (softened)

1 tablespoon (about 1.7 g) fresh rosemary

2 cloves (about 6 g) garlic

3.9 ounces (about 110 g) radicchio

Directions:

1. First, you finely mince the oregano, rosemary, and fresh basil.
2. After which you finely grate the garlic.
3. After that, you add the goat cheese, salt, herbs, garlic, and pepper to a mixing bowl.
4. This is when you combine well then set aside.
5. Furthermore, you cut the stem off the bottom of the radicchio. (NOTE: Carefully peel apart the leaves until you have 16 leaves for serving.) I prefer to use more of the inner leaves for their size and shape. Feel free to save any leftover radicchio for other salads or recipes. Wash and dry the leaves then.
6. Then, on each radicchio leave lay a piece of smoked salmon than a ½ ounce of the herbed goat cheese.
7. Finally, you sprinkle some black pepper on the top then serve.

Feta and Bacon Bites

Nutritional value:

Note: this makes a total of 24 servings of Feta and Bacon Bites.

Each serving

71.79 Calories

5.74g Fats

1.08g Net Carbs

3.66g Protein.

Ingredients:

2 cups of shredded mozzarella

¼ cup of crumbled feta cheese

Salt and pepper (to taste)

¾ cup of almond flour

8 slices bacon (cooked)

¼ cup chopped green onions

3 tablespoons of sriracha mayo (like Sarayo)

Directions:

1. Meanwhile, you heat your oven to 350°F
2. After which in a non-stick pan over medium heat, combine your almond flour and mozzarella; stir constantly.
3. Remember that the flour/cheese mix will form a dough like consistency after about 5 minutes.
4. After that, you place your dough between two pieces of parchment paper.
5. Then you roll flat with a rolling pin.
6. At this point, you use a cookie cutter or glass to cut out 24 circles. (NOTE: if you run out of dough then form the remaining bits into a ball.)
7. After that, you heat it up on the stove, then roll it out again.

8. This is when you place the circles of dough into your muffin tin (or on a cookie sheet.)
9. After which you top with the bacon, feta, and onions.
10. Then you bake at 350°F for about 15 minutes, until the edges are browned.
11. Finally, you cool, peel off the liners, and top with sriracha mayo!

Feta and Bacon Bites

Note: this makes a total of 24 servings of Feta and Bacon Bites.

Ingredients:

2 cups of shredded mozzarella

¼ cup of crumbled feta cheese

3 tablespoons of sriracha mayo (like Sarayo)

Salt and pepper (to taste)

¾ cup of almond flour

8 slices bacon (cooked)

¼ cup chopped green onions

Directions:

1. Meanwhile, you heat your oven to 350°F
2. After which, in a non-stick pan over medium heat, combine your almond flour and mozzarella; stir constantly.
3. Remember, the flour/cheese mix will form a dough like consistency after about 5 minutes.
4. After that, you place your dough between two pieces of parchment paper.
5. Then you roll flat with a rolling pin.
6. Furthermore, you use a cookie cutter or glass to cut out 24 circles. (NOTE: If you run out of dough, I suggest you form the remaining bits into a ball.)
7. After that, you heat it up on the stove, then roll it out again.
8. After which you place the circles of dough into your muffin tin (or on a cookie sheet.)
9. Then you top with the bacon, feta, and onions.
10. This is when you bake at 350°F for about 15 minutes until the edges are browned.
11. Finally, you cool, peel off the liners, and top with sriracha mayo!

Spicy Sausage Cheese Dip

Ingredients:

1 (about 15-ounce) can of Rotel Hot Diced Tomato (with Habaneros)

8 ounces of cream cheese

8 ounces of diced pepper jack cheese

1 pound of hot Italian ground sausage

¼ cup of sliced green onions

16 ounces of sour cream

Directions:

1. First, you use a saucepan, cook the hot Italian sausage on medium until lightly browned.
2. After which you stir in the can of Rotel and cook for a few minutes.
3. After that, you mix in the green onions and turn off the heat when the Italian sausage has fully browned.
4. Then you set a slow cooker on high then layer the bottom of the stoneware with the pepper jack cheese, and cream cheese cut into chunks.
5. At this point, you pour the Italian sausage on top of the cheese.
6. This is when you spread the sour cream on top of the Italian sausage.
7. Furthermore, after about an hour, stir the dip until the cheese is completely incorporated.
8. Allow to continue cooking, then after about two hours on high until the dip is completely done.

Jalapeno Popper Fat Bombs

Note: this makes a total of 3 Jalapeno Popper Fat Bombs.

Ingredients:

3 slices of Bacon

½ teaspoon of Dried Parsley

Salt and Pepper (to Taste)

3 oz. of Cream Cheese

1 medium Jalapeno Pepper

¼ teaspoon of Onion Powder

¼ teaspoon of Garlic Powder

Directions:

1. First, you fry 3 slices of bacon until crisp, set aside on paper towels; save bacon grease.
2. After which, you de-seed a jalapeno pepper, then dice into small pieces.
3. After that, you mix together with cream cheese, bacon fat, and spices; season to taste.
4. At this point, you crumble bacon and set on a plate.
5. Finally, you roll cream cheese mixture into balls using your hand, then roll the ball into the bacon.

Crispy Avocado Fries

Servings: 4

Ingredients

2 firm avocados (cut into ½-inch wedges)

¼ teaspoon of freshly ground black pepper

2 large eggs

2 tablespoons of Sriracha

Cooking spray, for greasing the baking sheet and spraying the avocado wedges

½ teaspoon of salt

⅓ cup of white whole-wheat flour

1 cup of whole-wheat panko breadcrumbs

⅓ cup of mayonnaise

Directions:

1. Meanwhile, heat the oven to 425°F.
2. After which you spray a rimmed baking sheet with cooking spray.
3. After that, season the avocados with salt and pepper.
4. At this point, place the flour, eggs, and panko in 3 separate dishes.
5. This is when you coat the avocado wedges in the flour, then dip in the egg; coat both sides with the panko.
6. Furthermore, place the wedges on the prepared baking sheet.
7. After that, coat both sides with cooking spray.
8. Then, bake for 30 minutes; flip the wedges halfway through.
9. In addition, whisk the mayonnaise and Sriracha in a small bowl.
10. Finally, serve the avocado fries with the aioli and enjoy!

Bacon Guac Bombs

Servings: 6

Ingredients:

½ large avocado

1 small chili pepper (chopped)

1 to 2 tablespoons of freshly chopped cilantro

¼ teaspoon of salt

½ small white onion (diced)

4 large slices bacon

¼ cup of unsalted, grass-fed butter

2 cloves garlic (crushed)

1 tablespoon of fresh lime juice

Freshly ground black pepper

Directions:

1. Meanwhile, heat the oven to 375°F.
2. After which you line a rimmed baking sheet with parchment paper.
3. After that, lay the bacon strips out flat.
4. Then place the baking sheet in the oven and cook for about 15 minutes, until the bacon is golden brown.
5. At this point, halve, de-seed, and peel the avocado.
6. This is when you place the butter, garlic, cilantro, avocado, chili pepper, and lime juice in a bowl and season with salt and pepper.
7. Furthermore, mash until well combined; add the diced onion and mix well.
8. After that, place in the refrigerator for 10 minutes.
9. In addition, crumble the bacon into small pieces.
10. After which you remove the guacamole mixture from the fridge and scoop out 6 balls.
11. Finally, roll each ball in the bacon crumbles and place on a dish; serve and enjoy!

Cabbage Chips

Servings: 6

Ingredients

1 large head cabbage

¼ cup of grated Parmesan cheese

2 teaspoons of extra-virgin olive oil

Kosher salt

Freshly ground black pepper

Directions:

1. Meanwhile, heat the oven to 250°F.
2. After which you set 2 wire racks inside 2 rimmed baking sheets.
3. After that, tear the cabbage leaves into large pieces, leaving out the thickest part of the ribs.
4. Then toss the cabbage leaves with the Parmesan and olive oil, then season with salt and pepper.
5. At this point, arrange in a single layer on wire racks.
6. This is where you bake for 35 minutes or until golden and crispy.
7. Finally, serve and enjoy!

Broccoli Cheesy Bread

Servings: 8

Ingredients

1 large egg

¼ cup of Parmesan cheese (grated)

½ teaspoon of dried oregano

Freshly ground black pepper

3 cups of broccoli (riced)

1½ cups of shredded mozzarella

2 cloves garlic (minced)

Kosher salt

Directions:

1. Meanwhile, heat the oven to 425°F and line a large rimmed baking sheet with parchment paper.
2. After which you place the riced broccoli in a large microwave-safe bowl.
3. After that, microwave, covered for 1 minute to steam.
4. Then, ring out the moisture from the broccoli using a paper towel.
5. At this point, transfer the broccoli to a large bowl and add the egg, 1 cup mozzarella, the Parmesan, and the garlic.
6. This is when you season with the salt, oregano, and pepper.
7. Furthermore, transfer the dough to the prepared baking sheet and shape into a thin, round crust.
8. After which you bake for 20 minutes or until golden.
9. Finally, top with remaining ½ cup mozzarella and bake for 10 more minutes or until the cheese is melted and the crust is crispy.
10. Then, serve and enjoy!

Pizza Chips

I prefer using Applegate turkey pepperoni because they don't add nitrates and are gluten free.

Servings: 7

Ingredients:

1½ cups of mozzarella cheese (shredded)

6 ounces of sliced pepperoni

Directions:

1. Meanwhile, heat the oven to 400°F.
2. After which on a rimmed baking sheet, arrange the pepperoni slices in batches of 4, close together.
3. After that, bake for 5 minutes; sprinkle the cheese on top.
4. At this point, you bake for another 3 minutes, or until the cheese is melted and crisp.
5. This is when you place the chips on paper towels and let cool for 5 minutes.
6. Then, serve and enjoy!

Celery Cream Cheese Boat

Servings: 4

Ingredients

1 teaspoon of everything bagel seasoning

10 stalks celery (rinsed)

2 (1-ounce) packages cream cheese

Directions:

1. First, cut the celery stalks into 3 sections each.
2. After which you stuff the celery with the cream cheese.
3. After that, sprinkle the stalks with everything bagel seasoning.
4. Then, serve and enjoy!

Super Trail Mix

Servings: 6

Ingredients

½ cup of whole almonds, raw

½ cup of walnut pieces

¼ cup of chia seeds

½ cup of coconut oil (melted)

¼ cup of Cruise Control–friendly sweetener

½ cup of almond slices

½ cup of pecan halves

½ cup of coconut flakes (unsweetened)

¼ cup of flaxseeds

1 tablespoon of ground cinnamon

1 teaspoon of Himalayan pink salt

Directions:

1. Meanwhile, heat the oven to 350°F.
2. After which you line a rimmed baking sheet with parchment paper.
3. After which, in a large bowl, combine the whole almonds, walnuts, pecans, sliced almonds, chia seeds, coconut flakes, and flaxseeds.
4. At this point, you add the coconut oil to the mix.
5. Then you sprinkle in the cinnamon and salt; mix well.
6. Furthermore, place the mixture on the prepared baking sheet and bake for 15 minutes.
7. This is when you let the trail mix cool for 30 minutes.
8. Finally, sprinkle with the Cruise Control–friendly sweetener, serve, and enjoy.

Cauliflower Cheese Muffins

Servings: 8

Ingredients:

1 large cauliflower (chopped)

2 ounces of cream cheese

Freshly ground black pepper (to taste)

2 large eggs (beaten)

Non-stick cooking spray (for greasing the muffin pan)

1 cup of heavy cream

½ teaspoon of onion powder

1¾ cups of shredded sharp Cheddar cheese

Directions:

1. Meanwhile, heat the oven to 350°F.
2. After which you spray a muffin tin with non-stick spray.
3. After that, bring a large pot of water to a boil over medium-high heat.
4. Then, add the cauliflower and boil until tender, about 7 to 10 minutes. Drain.
5. At this point, you cook the cream and cream cheese in a medium saucepan over low heat until creamy, about 5 minutes, stirring constantly.
6. This is when you add the onion powder and pepper.
7. Furthermore, add 1 cup shredded Cheddar, the eggs, and the cauliflower to the mixture and stir until smooth.
8. After which you spoon into the prepared muffin tin and sprinkle with the remaining ¾ cup shredded Cheddar and bake for 20 minutes.
9. Then you cool for 15 minutes before removing from the muffin pan.
10. Finally, serve and enjoy!

BOOST ZONE DESSERTS

Pumpkin Snickerdoodle Cookies

Nutritional value:

Note: this makes a total of 15 Pumpkin Snickerdoodle Cookies.

Ingredients:

The Cookies

¼ cup of Butter (salted)

1 teaspoon of Vanilla Extract

1 large Egg

25 drops of Liquid Stevia

1 ½ cups of Almond Flour

½ cup of Pumpkin Puree

½ teaspoon of Baking Powder

¼ cup of Erythritol

The Topping:

2 teaspoons of Erythritol

1 teaspoon of Pumpkin Pie Spice

Directions:

1. Meanwhile, you heat oven to 350F.
2. After which you measure out dry ingredients and mix.
3. Then in a separate container, you measure out the butter, pumpkin puree, vanilla, and liquid stevia.
4. At this point, you mix everything together well until a pastry dough is formed.

5. After that, you roll the dough into small balls and set on a cookie sheet covered with a Silpat. (NOTE: About 15 cookies in total.)
6. Furthermore, you press the balls flat with your hand (or the bottom side of a jar) and bake for about 12-13 minutes.
7. Finally, while the cookies are cooking, run 2 teaspoons of erythritol and 1 teaspoon of pumpkin pie spice through a spice grinder.
8. Once the cookies are done, I suggest you sprinkle with the topping and let cool completely.

Easy Strawberry Shortcakes

Note: this makes a total of 5 Strawberry Shortcakes.

Ingredients:

Puff Cakes

3 oz. of Cream Cheese

2 tablespoons of Erythritol

3 large Eggs

¼ teaspoon of Baking Powder

½ teaspoon of Vanilla Extract

Filling

1 cup of Heavy Cream

10 medium Strawberries

Directions:

1. Meanwhile, you heat oven to 300F.
2. After which you separate the egg whites from the yolks.
3. After that, start by beating the egg whites until they are fluffy.
4. Then in the container with the yolks, add cream cheese, vanilla, baking powder, and erythritol and beat until smooth.
5. At this point, you fold egg whites slowly into the egg yolk mixture, then spread evenly on a baking sheet with a Silpat.
6. Finally, you bake for about 25-30 minutes.
7. This is when you let cool, then sandwich whipped cream and strawberries between 2 cakes.

Vanilla Cream Cheese Frosting

Ingredients:

¼ cup of powdered erythritol

½ teaspoon of vanilla extract

4 ounces of cream cheese

3 tablespoons of heavy whipping cream

Directions:

1. Meanwhile, you heat oven to 350° F while gathering your ingredients.
2. After which, in a medium sized bowl, mix the eggs, mayonnaise, and vanilla bean paste.
3. If you want the batter to be really smooth, I suggest you use a hand mixer.
4. After that, you set the bowl to the side.
5. Then in another bowl, mix together the almond flour, erythritol, salt, and baking powder.
6. At this point, you slowly whisk the batter into the almond flour. (NOTE: if you have a hard time mixing them together, I suggest you use the hand blender until it is smooth.)
7. However, the mixture will seem a little dry when it's mixed, but this is normal.
8. Furthermore, using a ¼ cup measure, spoon out eight servings into a lined muffin or cupcake pan.
9. Finally, you bake for 20-25 minutes at 350° F or until they're lightly browned on top.
10. Make sure you frost after they have cooled.

Chai Spice Mug Cake

Ingredients:

Base

2 tablespoons of butter

1 tablespoon of erythritol

½ teaspoon of baking powder

1 large egg

2 tablespoons of almond flour

7 drops of liquid Stevia

Flavor

¼ teaspoon of cinnamon

¼ teaspoon of clove

¼ teaspoon of vanilla extract

2 tablespoons of almond flour

¼ teaspoon of ginger

¼ teaspoon of cardamom

Directions:

1. First, you mix all room temperature ingredients together in a mug.
2. After which you microwave on high for 70 seconds.
3. After that, you turn the cup upside down and lightly bang it against a plate.
4. **Optional:** feel free to top with whipped cream and sprinkle of cinnamon.

Italian Lemon Sponge Cake

Note: this made a total of 3 cakes.

Cut the cakes into halves or make them in a cupcake for easy serving!

Ingredients:

Italian Sponge Cake

1 teaspoon of Baking Powder

5 large Eggs (Separated)

1 teaspoon of Almond Extract

¼ teaspoon of Liquid Stevia

½ teaspoon of Cream of Tartar (for egg whites)

1 cup of Honey Ville Almond Flour

¼ teaspoon of Salt

1 teaspoon of Vanilla

¼ cup of NOW Erythritol

Zest ½ Lemon

2 tablespoons of Olive Oil

Raspberry Lemon Icing

Ingredients:

4 tablespoons of Heavy Cream

Juice ½ Lemon

4 tablespoons of Butter

1/3 cup of Fresh Raspberries

Directions:

1. Meanwhile, you heat oven to 325F.
2. After which you mix all dry ingredients together (EXCEPT cream of tartar), then mix all wet ingredients together (EXCEPT egg whites and lemon zest).
3. After that, you whip egg whites in a small mixing bowl with the cream of tartar and lemon zest until still peaks form.
4. Then you aggressively fold 1/3 egg white mixture into batter.
5. This is when you add the rest and gently fold it in.
6. At this point, you pour batter among cupcake molds or cake molds and bake for 25 minutes.
7. Then, while the cake is cooking, heat butter until it starts to brown.
8. Add cream and lemon juice and remove from heat while you continue stirring.
9. After which you add raspberries and lightly mash with a fork into the frosting.
10. Let cool for about10-15 minutes.
11. Finally, ice cake and serve!

Low Carb Cookie Butter

Note: this makes about 1 cup of Low Carb Cookie Butter.

Ingredients:

¾ cup of Raw Cashews

¼ teaspoon of Cinnamon

1/8 teaspoon of Nutmeg

2 tablespoons of Butter

Pinch Salt

1 cup of Raw Macadamias

1 teaspoon of Vanilla

¼ teaspoon of Ginger

1/8 teaspoon of Cloves

2 tablespoons of Heavy Cream

2 tablespoons of Swerve (powdered)

Directions:

1. First, you add macadamia nuts and cashews into food processor and process until smooth.
2. After which you brown the butter with the powdered Swerve in a saucepan.
3. Then once butter is brown, add heavy cream and stir into the butter.
4. After that, you remove from heat.
5. At this point, you add vanilla and spices, then process again until well combined and little to no lumps inside.

NOTE: While processing, pour in caramel sauce and continue the process until you're happy with the consistency.

LC Peanut Butter Meringue Cookies

Nutritional value: this makes a total of 18 servings of Peanut Butter Meringue Cookies.

Ingredients:

2 tablespoons of sweetener

1 cup of egg whites (room temp)

½ cup of creamy peanut butter

Directions:

1. Meanwhile, you heat oven to 200°F.
2. After which you beat egg whites on high speed till soft peaks form.
3. After that, you turn the speed down and while beating slowly add sweetener.
4. Then you add peanut butter and mix on low speed till combined.
5. At this point, you place 2 Tablespoons of meringue on parchment- or Silpat-covered baking sheet.
6. After that, you bake for 1 hour without opening the oven door.
7. Finally, you turn oven off and leave cookies in the oven for an additional hour.

Lemon & Rosemary Low Carb Shortbread

Note: this makes a total of 24 servings of Lemon & Rosemary Low Carb Shortbread.

Ingredients:

2 cups of almond flour

1 tablespoon of freshly grated lemon zest

1 teaspoon of vanilla extract

½ teaspoon of baking powder

6 tablespoons of butter

1/3 cup of granulated Splenda (or better still another granulated sweetener)

4 teaspoons of squeezed lemon juice

2 teaspoons of rosemary

½ teaspoon of baking soda

Directions:

1. First, you measure out 2 cups of almond flour, ½ teaspoon baking powder, and ½ teaspoon baking soda in a large mixing bowl.
2. After which you add 1/3 cup Splenda or another granulated sweetener to the mixture; set aside.
3. After that, you zest your lemon with a micro plane until you have 1 Tablespoon of lemon zest. (NOTE: Juice half the lemon to get 4teaspoon lemon juice.)
4. Then in the microwave, melt 6 Tablespoons of butter and then add 1 teaspoon vanilla extract.
5. At this point, you transfer your almond flour and sweetener to a small mixing bowl.
6. After that, you put your butter, lemon zest, lemon juice, and chopped rosemary into the now empty large mixing bowl.
7. After which you add your almond flour back into the wet mixture slowly, stirring as you go.
8. Make sure you keep mixing until all the almond flour is added back.
9. This is when you wrap the dough tightly in plastic wrap.

10. Furthermore, you place the wrapped dough in the freezer for 30 minutes, or until hard.
11. Meanwhile, you heat your oven to 350F, remove your dough, and unwrap it.
12. After which you cut your dough in ~1/2" increments with a sharp knife. NOTE: If this knife isn't sharp, it will make the dough crumble. If the dough is still crumbling, it implies that it needs more time in the freezer.
13. Then you grease a cookie sheet with SALTED butter and place your cookies on it.
14. Finally, you bake for about 15 minutes at 350 degrees.
15. Once removed, I suggest you allow to cool for 10 minutes, remove from cookie sheet, and enjoy!

Notes

For me; I used dried rosemary, but fresh would be even better.

Coconut Peanut Butter Balls

Ingredients:

3 teaspoons of unsweetened cocoa powder

½ cup of unsweetened coconut flakes

3 tablespoons of creamy peanut butter

2 ½ teaspoons of powdered erythritol

2 teaspoons of almond flour

Directions:

1. First, you mix together your peanut butter, cocoa, erythritol, and flour, in a bowl.
2. After which you freeze for one hour.
3. Using a melon baller (or better still small spoon), spoon out a small serving of the peanut butter mix.
4. After that, you drop it into your coconut flakes and roll around with your hands so the coconut covers the ball. (NOTE: Reshape into a ball if needed.)
5. Finally, you refrigerate overnight so they firm up.

Cream Cheese Truffles

Ingredients:

½ cup of unsweetened cocoa powder (divided)

¼ teaspoon of liquid Stevia

1 tablespoon of instant coffee

24 paper candy cups (for serving)

16 ounces' cream cheese (softened)

4 tablespoons of Swerve confectioners

½ teaspoon of rum extract

2 tablespoons of water

1 tablespoon of heavy whipping cream

Directions:

1. First, in a large bowl add the cream cheese, ¼ cup of cocoa powder, rum extract, instant coffee, Swerve, Stevia, water, and heavy whipping cream.
2. After which you use an electric hand mixer to whip all of the ingredients together until they are well combined.
3. After that, you place the bowl in the fridge for half an hour to chill before rolling.
4. Then you spread the remaining ¼ cup cocoa powder out.
5. At this point, you roll heaping tablespoons in the palm of your hand to form balls, then roll them around in the cocoa powder. (NOTE: You will end up with about 24 total.)
6. Finally, you place them individually in small paper candy cups.
7. Make sure you chill for an hour before serving.

Chocolate Salted Peanut Butter Cups

Servings: 6

Ingredients:

Chocolate Coating

3 tablespoons of Swerve Confectioner's sweetener

6 tablespoons of coconut oil (melted)

6 tablespoons of unsweetened cocoa powder

Peanut Butter Filling

2 teaspoons of no-sugar-added peanut butter

½ teaspoon of kosher salt (or better still sea salt)

2 tablespoons of cocoa butter (melted)

1 tablespoon of Swerve Confectioner's sweetener

Directions:

1. First, place muffin liners in 6 cups of a muffin tin; set aside.
2. After which you whisk together the coconut oil, cocoa powder, and Swerve in a medium bowl.
3. After that, place a tablespoon of chocolate mixture in each muffin liner.
4. At this point, place in the freezer for 5 minutes.
5. Then, in a separate, microwave-safe bowl, whisk together the cocoa butter, peanut butter, Swerve, and salt.
6. Furthermore, once combined, microwave on high for 10 seconds.
7. After that, remove the chocolate from the freezer and add 1½ teaspoons of the peanut butter mixture to the frozen chocolate coating.
8. This is when you return to the freezer for another 3 minutes.
9. In addition, remove from the freezer and add 1 tablespoon of the remaining chocolate in each cup, covering the peanut butter mixture.
10. After which you freeze again for 5 minutes; then eat and enjoy.
11. You can store in fridge or freezer in an airtight storage container. (NOTE: let soften for 15 to 20 minutes before eating; if desired.

Snap Cookie Ice-Cream Slider

Servings: 6

Ingredients:

12 Keto-Snap cookies

6 ounces of low-sugar (or better still non-dairy ice cream)

Directions:

1. First, place about 2 tablespoons of ice cream on the bottom of a cookie and spread to the edge.
2. After which you top with another cookie.
3. After that, repeat to make 6 ice-cream sliders.
4. Then, serve and enjoy!

Chocolate Avocado Pops

Servings: 10

Ingredients:

⅓ cup of lime juice

¾ cup of coconut milk

1 tablespoon of coconut oil

3 ripe avocados

3 tablespoons of Cruise Control–friendly sweetener

1 cup of dark chocolate chips (55% cocoa)

Directions:

1. First, in the bowl of a blender, combine lime juice, avocados, sweetener, and coconut milk.
2. After which you blend until smooth and pour into popsicle molds.
3. After that, freeze for 6 hours or overnight, until the molds are firm.
4. Then, in a medium microwave-safe bowl, combine the dark chocolate chips and coconut oil.
5. At this point, microwave until melted, then let cool to room temperature.
6. Finally, dunk the frozen pops in the chocolate and serve.

Chocolate Pudding

Servings: 2

Ingredients

2 ounces of plain full-fat triple-cream yogurt (Peak Yogurt)

¼ cup of Cruise Control–friendly sweetener

¼ teaspoon of pure vanilla extract

1 overripe avocado, large

¼ cup of unsweetened cocoa powder

1½ teaspoons of cinnamon

¼ teaspoon of cayenne pepper

Directions:

1. First, place all of the ingredients in a blender and process until smooth.
2. Then you spoon into 2 bowls and enjoy!

Note: remember, you can use other whole-fat plain yogurts, but I prefer Peak Yogurt because it is designed to be lower in sugar, so more Cruise Control–friendly.

Million-Dollar Milkshake

Servings: 1

Ingredients:

1 tablespoon of raw cashew butter

1 teaspoon of raw cacao powder

1 tablespoon of Cruise Control–friendly sweetener

½ cup of unsweetened almond milk

1 scoop grass-fed vanilla whey protein

1 teaspoon of chia seeds

1 tablespoon of MCT oil

Directions:

1. First, place all of the ingredients in a blender.
2. Then, blend until and smooth.

Chocolate Macadamia Nut Parfait

Servings: 1

Ingredients

2 tablespoons of macadamia nuts

5 ounces plain full-fat triple-cream yogurt

1 (1-ounce) packet of FBOMB Salted Chocolate Macadamia Nut Butter

Directions:

1. First, open a 5-ounce container of natural, full-fat yogurt and squeeze a packet of FBOMB Salted Chocolate Macadamia Nut Butter into it.
2. After that, stir and top with macadamia nuts.
3. Then, serve and enjoy!

Almond Butter Cookies

Servings: 15

Ingredients

½ cup of Cruise Control–friendly sweetener

1 teaspoon of pure vanilla extract

½ teaspoon of ground cinnamon

1 cup of natural almond butter

1 large egg

¼ teaspoon of sea salt

Directions:

1. Meanwhile, heat the oven to 350°F.
2. After which you line a baking sheet with parchment paper.
3. Then, in a large bowl, mix together the almond butter and sweetener until smooth.
4. At this point, mix in the vanilla, egg, salt, and cinnamon and stir until well combined.
5. This is when you scoop into 15 cookies.
6. Furthermore, place the dough balls on the prepared baking sheet 2 inches apart, and then use a fork to flatten them and form a crisscross pattern.
7. After that, bake for 12 minutes or until the cookies are slightly browned on the bottom.
8. Finally, cool on the baking sheet for 3 minutes.
9. Then, serve and enjoy!

Double Fudge Brownies

Servings: 16

Ingredients

½ cup of unsalted grass-fed butter (melted)

3 large eggs

½ cup of almond flour

1 tablespoon of gelatin

⅓ cup of dark chocolate chips (55% cocoa)

Nonstock cooking spray (for greasing the pan)

⅔ cup of Cruise Control–friendly sweetener

½ teaspoon of pure vanilla extract

⅓ cup of cocoa powder

½ teaspoon of baking powder

¼ teaspoon of salt

Directions:

1. Meanwhile, heat the oven to 350°F.
2. After which you grease an 8 x 8-inch baking pan with non-stick cooking spray.
3. Then, in a large bowl, whisk together the butter, eggs, sweetener, and vanilla.
4. At this point, add the cocoa powder, baking powder, almond flour, gelatin, and salt and whisk until well combined.
5. This is when you stir in ¼ cup water to thin the batter.
6. Furthermore, stir in the chocolate chips.
7. After that, spread the batter in the prepared baking pan.
8. In addition, bake for 15 minutes, until the edges are set.
9. Finally, remove and let cool completely in the pan.
10. Then, serve and enjoy!

Churro Mug Cake

Servings: 1

Ingredients

2 tablespoons of butter

1 tablespoon of Cruise Control–friendly sweetener

½ teaspoon of baking powder

¼ teaspoon of nutmeg

Whipped cream (it is optional)

1 large egg

2 tablespoons of almond flour

7 drops of liquid stevia

¼ teaspoon of cinnamon, plus more for serving

¼ teaspoon of pure vanilla extract

Directions:

1. First, mix together the butter, sweetener, baking powder, nutmeg, egg, almond flour, liquid stevia, cinnamon, and vanilla in a microwavable mug.
2. After which you microwave on high for 1 minute.
3. After that, turn the mug upside down on a plate and remove the cake.
4. Then, top with whipped cream, if using, and a dash of cinnamon.
5. Finally, serve and enjoy!

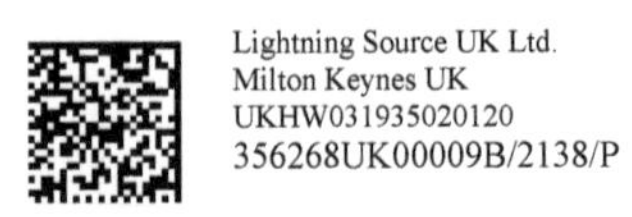

Lightning Source UK Ltd.
Milton Keynes UK
UKHW031935020120
356268UK00009B/2138/P